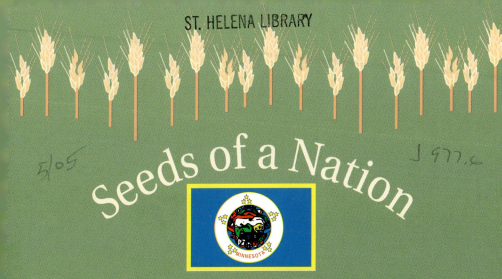

Seeds of a Nation

Minnesota

P. M. Boekhoff
Stuart A. Kallen

KidHaven Press, an imprint of Gale Group, Inc.
10911 Technology Place, San Diego, CA 92127

On Cover: Fort Snelling.

Library of Congress Cataloging-in-Publication Data
Boekhoff, P. M. (Patti Marlene), 1957–
    Minnesota / by P. M. Boekhoff and Stuart A. Kallen.
        p. cm. — (Seeds of a Nation)
    Includes bibliographical references and index.
    Summary: Discusses the early history of Minnesota from the indige-
nous Native Americans through European exploration and settlement,
to statehood in 1858.
    ISBN 0–7377–1021–7 (hardback: alk. paper)
    1. Minnesota—History—To 1858—Juvenile literature. [1. Minnesota—
History—To 1858.] I. Kallen, Stuart A., 1955- II. Title. III. Series.
    F606 .B695 2002
    977.6—dc21

                                    2001002966

Picture Credits
Cover Photo: Minnesota Historical Society
S. Holmes Andrews/Minnesota Historical Society, 33
© Bettmann/CORBIS, 17, 19, 27
© Christie's Images/CORBIS, 13, 21
Seth Eastman/Minnesota Historical Society, 8
© Historical Picture Archive/CORBIS, 29
Hulton/Archive by Getty Images, 10, 14, 36, 37
Chris Juoan, 5, 7, 22, 24
Monroe P. Killy/Minnesota Historical Society, 25
© Lake County Museum/CORBIS, 41
© Francis G. Mayer/CORBIS, 11, 28
Frank Blackwell Mayer/Minnesota Historical Society, 38
Minnesota Historical Society, 32
© Minnesota Historical Society/CORBIS, 31
© Richard Hamilton Smith/CORBIS, 16, 39
© Joseph Sohm; ChromoSohm Inc./CORBIS, 42
Edwin Whitefield/Minnesota Historical Society, 6

Copyright 2002 by KidHaven Press, an imprint of Gale Group, Inc.
        10911 Technology Place, San Diego, California 92127

Printed in the U.S.A.

Contents

Chapter One

Dakota Culture

Minnesota is a state in the upper Midwest region of the United States. It is bordered by Canada to the north, Lake Superior and Wisconsin to the east, Iowa to the south, and North and South Dakota to the west. Its capital is Saint Paul, and its largest city is Minneapolis. These two cities border each other and are called the Twin Cities.

The first people known to live in Minnesota were part of the Mississippian culture. These people mined copper along the shores of Lake Superior about six thousand years ago. Scientists believe that these early Minnesotans were the first people in the world to use copper to make tools and weapons.

The Mississippians also carved and painted pictures on large rocks. One area near the present-day town of Jeffers has about two thousand such pictures of animals, people, and activities that tell the story of the

Mississippians' lives long ago.

Around 500 B.C., these native people began building giant earth mounds shaped like animals such as bears, birds, buffalo, and snakes. In all, the Mississippians created more than ten thousand of these mounds throughout Minnesota. They contain art objects and the bones of buried people, leading researchers to believe that the sites were used as graves and centers of worship.

MINNESOTA'S PLACE IN THE UNITED STATES TODAY

The Dakota tribe built giant earth mounds as graves and centers of worship.

The Dakota

Eventually the Mound Building culture developed into the Dakota tribe, who lived in the forests and grasslands of Minnesota. The Dakota are also known today as the Santee Sioux. This name means "little snakes," and was given to them by their French enemies in the eighteenth century. Naturally, the tribes prefer to be called Dakota, a way of saying "friends" or "allies" in their language.

Before European contact, the Dakota were part of a large group of tribes who called themselves Seven Council Fires (Oceti Sakowin). Four of the seven

Council groups lived in present-day Minnesota. They were the People of Spirit Lake (Mdewakanton), Dwellers Among the Leaves (Wahpeton), Shooters Among the Leaves (Wahpekute), and People of the Swamp (Sisseton).

All these tribes lived in a similar manner, building villages along rivers and lakes. Dakota villages were full of sturdy wooden houses made of elm posts covered with elm bark panels about six feet square. The houses were

built by women, with men helping to put the bark panels on the roofs. Most houses were large, providing shelter for extended families of twenty-five people or more.

The Woodland Harvest

Women planted and harvested gardens of corn, beans, and squash near their homes. Wild foods were also very plentiful, and people gathered blackberries, cherries, cranberries, and huckleberries. These foods were eaten raw, made into cakes, or mixed with other ingredients to add flavor. Hardy plants such as lily roots,

Houses in Dakota villages were made of elm posts and elm bark panels.

beans, potatoes, and turnips were a few of the many foods harvested from the wild.

Women also harvested sap from maple and box elder trees every spring. The liquid was boiled down to make sugar, sweet syrup, and medicine. Sap from ash and birch trees made a bitter syrup that was also used for medicine.

Hunting Buffalo

Each summer, the Dakota left their wooden homes to hunt in the prairie grasslands of southwestern Minnesota where millions of buffalo lived. During the hunting trips, the Dakota stayed in lightweight tepees made from buffalo hides that were cured and sewn together by women.

Before Europeans brought horses to the area, Dakota men and boys hunted on foot, hiding in brush and shooting the animals with bows and arrows. After the hunt, each part of the buffalo was used for food, clothing, or shelter. The meat was roasted and eaten immediately or dried in the sun to make buffalo jerky that could be eaten later.

Buffalo hides were used to make moccasins, leggings, shirts, jackets, dresses, vests, gloves, and blankets. The hooves were used to make glue, and the tough muscle called sinew was rolled into a strong rope. Bones were shaped into tools such as plows, hammers, and even sewing needles.

Buffalo hides were used for moccasins, clothing, and blankets.

Summer Council Meetings

Every summer after the buffalo hunt, families from each of the four Dakota Council Fires traveled to South Dakota to form the Seven Council Fires with the Lakota and Nakota Councils.

The tribes met in the sacred Black Hills in South Dakota. These councils were social events where the tribes traded news and gifts. After a long, grueling buffalo hunt people were eager to play. People competed against one another in wrestling matches, archery contests, and foot races. Councils were also religious events marked by many ceremonies held to give thanks for the past year, and offer prayers for help in the coming year.

At the Seven Council meetings, the Dakota were known as medical healers among the other tribes. In fact they were called the People of the Herbs because Dakota medicine men and women used their knowledge of plants to prevent illnesses such as infection, toothaches, and colds. They also could set broken bones.

The summer buffalo hunt drew Dakota from all over the region.

Harvesting Wild Rice

After the council was over, the Dakota returned home in late summer to fish and to harvest the wild rice that grew in abundance in Minnesota's marshy lakes.

Women harvested the wild rice using birchbark canoes. To obtain the grain, they would paddle out to the middle of a lake and use a wooden rod to lightly hit the plants. This loosened the wild rice so that it fell onto the floor of their canoes. Most of the rice was taken back to the village, but some was buried underground for use during emergencies.

Hunting and Fishing

While women harvested rice for the family, men used their canoes to hunt on the lakes. Using bows, arrows, and snares they caught birds such as cranes, ducks, geese, and loons.

When not hunting birds, Dakota men caught fish using a variety of methods. Fish could be shot with an arrow or spear. They could be caught with a hook attached to fishing lines spun from hemp or animal sinew. To catch fish in streams, men dammed the river with fish traps made from twigs and rope. As the fish were pushed downstream by the current, they would become ensnared in the traps.

In the long, bitterly cold Minnesota winters, families moved to the forests, which covered almost two-thirds of the land. The tall trees sheltered the tepees from the cold winter winds.

Birchbark canoes were used to harvest wild rice.

It was necessary to catch food even on the coldest winter days. Usually men could catch fish by cutting holes into the ice that had formed over the frozen lakes and rivers. When the fish swam under the holes in the ice, fishermen caught them with hooks, spears, or arrows attached to long fishing lines.

In the forests the Dakota men hunted bear, deer, elk, moose, muskrat and beaver for their warm fur, and for meat to eat with wild rice and dried foods.

After dinner, families gathered around the warm fire in the tepee to sing and tell stories. Boys and girls listened as their elders told tales about their history, traditions, and religion. Children were taught that no

Dakota men cut holes in the frozen rivers to catch fish with hooks, spears, or arrows.

person was more important than the tribe, and that by taking care of the well-being of the tribe, each person would also be taken care of.

The Dakota people based their lives on the rhythm of the changing seasons. They hunted and harvested only what they needed, while living in a land of natural abundance. This region full of almost limitless natural resources would soon attract others. Their lives would change forever.

Chapter Two

The Fur Traders

The names of the first European explorers to reach present-day Minnesota are unknown but some believe that they left a record of their visit.

In 1898, an ancient slab of stone, called the Kensington runestone, was found in Kensington, Minnesota. The stone was marked with ancient Northern European letters, called runes, and dated 1362. It tells of the journey of thirty explorers who came to America and journeyed to Minnesota.

Although many researchers have studied the Kensington runestone, no one has been able to prove that it is real, or a fake carved by a local nineteenth-century farmer. Some people think it is a genuine record of European travelers, others think it is a hoax.

The first known Europeans to travel to Minnesota were French explorers Pierre Esprit Radisson and his brother-in-law Médard Chouart, sieur des Groseilliers.

The Kensington runestone tells of explorers passing through Minnesota.

These men, who had already explored present-day Canada, came to the region in 1660 in search of animal furs. The Dakota treated these newcomers as friends, giving them large supplies of corn, wild rice, and meat.

The French wanted the Dakota to supply them with furs from beavers, otters, and muskrat. The pelts would be shipped to France to be made into hats and fur collars which were a part of a growing fashion fad in Europe at that time. In return the Dakota tribes would receive European goods such as hatchets, kettles, knives, nails, and scissors. Dakota women would receive heavy wool fabric to make warm clothing. In addition men would receive liquor along with guns and ammunition for hunting beaver and muskrat.

Conflict with Newcomers

The Dakota agreed to trade, and Radisson and des Groseilliers returned to their base in Montreal, Canada, with canoes laden with furs. When French officials heard Radisson's description of the Dakota, they sent Catholic priests to Minnesota to strengthen the new friendship

Pierre Esprit Radisson is one of the first known Europeans to explore Minnesota.

between the Europeans and the Native Americans. In the following years, French explorers, traders, missionaries, and soldiers increased their visits to Dakota villages.

By the 1670s, another group of outsiders came to the land of the Dakota. The Ojibwa tribe, who previously lived in present-day Illinois, Wisconsin, and southern Canada moved to northern Minnesota. This began a series of bitter conflicts with the Dakota that would last for nearly two hundred years.

Fur Trade Negotiations

In 1679, Daniel Greysolon, sieur Duluth traveled to Minnesota to convince the Dakota to make peace with the Ojibwa. Duluth hoped to **negotiate** a peace that would protect the French fur trade from disruption of war.

Duluth met a group of Dakota at the present site of the town of Duluth and traveled inland to their large village on the south shore of Lake Mille Lacs in central Minnesota. There he held a council with the Dakota and the Ojibwa, but he could not negotiate a peace between the warring tribes. Duluth was, however, able to help open trade between the French and the Ojibwa.

By 1700, the British had also come to Minnesota, eager to profit by trading furs with the Native Americans. The Minnesota River Valley became the gateway for Europeans expanding into the western plains as well as an important water route for the fur trade. Both the English and the French built trading posts along this waterway attempting to control the fur trade in the area.

Many Dakota burial ceremonies (pictured) resulted from wars with the Ojibwa tribe.

Competition between France and England led the two European powers to establish military and trading alliances with the Native Americans. Each worked to gain a **monopoly** on trade with different tribes. By favoring one tribe over another, the French and English created conflicts between the Dakota and Ojibwa and warfare between the tribes increased.

By this time, the Dakota were outnumbered by the Ojibwa, who were kept well-supplied with guns by the French military. With greater firepower and more warriors, the Ojibwa won a series of military victories over the Dakota people.

After suffering a series of bitter defeats over the course of forty years, the Dakota were finally forced from their homelands and pushed into the prairies of central and southern Minnesota. The Ojibwa gained control of the woodlands, lakes, and rivers of northern Minnesota.

The French and Indian War

By the time the Dakota were defeated, the French and English were fighting a series of conflicts in the Great Lakes area to find out who would finally control North America. In 1754, the scattered conflicts erupted into the French and Indian War, a series of battles fought by the two European powers and their Native American allies in the eastern half of the United States.

When France realized it might lose the war in 1762, it gave its land west of the Mississippi, including parts of present-day Minnesota, to Spain. The next year France gave its remaining North American land, including northern Minnesota east of the Mississippi River, to Great Britain under the Treaty of Paris.

The British Influence

After 1763, the British controlled the northeastern part of Minnesota. In 1766, Englishman Jonathan Carver visited the Dakota villages in Minnesota to arrange for a British takeover of the French fur trading networks in the region. During his travels, Carver wrote the first English book about the Native Americans in the area.

As trade increased, the British built forts at many of the river junctions in the area. From these forts, they were able to control the canoes and boats carrying furs along the river trade routes. By allowing only British boats to pass, they controlled the entire fur trade in Minnesota.

To keep peace with the Native Americans who lived around the Great Lakes, the British promised to keep American settlers from moving west of the Appalachian Mountains in Pennsylvania, Ohio, and West Virginia.

While the British were taking over the fur trade in the Midwest, American colonists along the East Coast were starting a revolution to break free of British control. In 1775, the American Revolution began pitting Americans against their British rulers.

One of the causes of the revolution was the British policy preventing settlement west of the Appalachian Mountains. When the war broke out, American rebels ignored the British laws and moved to outposts along the Mississippi River in present-day Minnesota.

The British built forts with fur trading posts for the growing trade with the Native Americans.

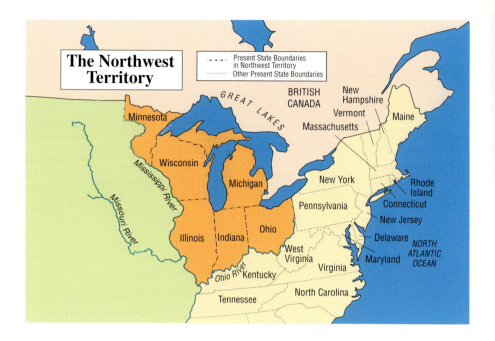

The Northwest Territory

····· Present State Boundaries in Northwest Territory
·········· Other Present State Boundaries

GREAT LAKES

BRITISH CANADA

Minnesota

Wisconsin

Mississippi River

Missouri River

Michigan

Illinois Indiana Ohio

Ohio River Kentucky

Tennessee

New Hampshire
Vermont
Massachusetts
Maine

New York

Pennsylvania

Rhode Island
Connecticut
New Jersey
Delaware
Maryland

West Virginia
Virginia

North Carolina

NORTH ATLANTIC OCEAN

Because the British wished to keep the American rebels out of Dakota territory, they won a powerful Dakota ally. Wabasha, chief of the People of Spirit Lake (Mdewakanton), became a well-respected general in the American Revolution. General Wabasha led hundreds of Dakota warriors against American rebels who lived along the Mississippi River. In spite of this victory, the British lost the American Revolution in battles along the East Coast in 1783.

After the war, Great Britain lost its claims to the part of Minnesota east of the Mississippi River. Although the new country called the United States gained independence, British fur traders continued to operate throughout Minnesota until the American traders arrived in the area in the next century.

Chapter Three

U.S. Settlement

In 1800, Minnesota was home to several conflicting groups who had claims upon the land. The French had bought back the area west of the Mississippi River that it had given to Spain in 1762. British fur traders, however, continued to work in the area. And the Dakota and Ojibwa tribes were not ready to surrender their ancient homeland to European interests.

In 1803, the United States bought the Minnesota region from France as part of the Louisiana Purchase, which more than doubled the size of the United States.

Minnesota was now part of the United States, but the British remained in control of the fur trade. In 1805, the U.S. government sent Lieutenant Zebulon Montgomery Pike and a small army up the Mississippi River to warn British traders that they were trespassing on U.S. territory.

Pike's Treaty

Pike's mission also involved buying land from the Dakota tribe so the U.S. government could build forts and trading posts in the area. Seven Dakota leaders from the People of Spirit Lake Council met with Pike. The lieutenant asked the leaders to sign a treaty giving the U.S. government one hundred thousand acres of land at the junction of the Mississippi and Saint Croix Rivers in the eastern part of the state. This land was located where the Mississippi and Minnesota Rivers meet just south of present-day Minneapolis.

The treaty did not mention the amount of money to be paid to the Dakota. But Pike promised the council members that the government would pay them at least two hundred thousand dollars. Only two of the seven leaders in one Dakota council group agreed to the sale. In spite of this, the U.S. government insisted the treaty was legal.

The U.S. senate approved the treaty, making it law. The treaty awarded the Dakota people two thousand dollars for their land, about 1 percent of the minimum amount promised. The Dakota did not receive this reduced sum until 1819, when the United States began constructing a huge stone **fortress** on the treaty land.

The meeting between the Dakota and Pike's council is staged for a photograph.

American Military Presence

Traders of the American Fur Company, owned by millionaire John Jacob Astor, led the American advance into Minnesota. The traders were followed by a U.S. Army **detachment** led by Colonel Josiah Snelling. Snelling built a diamond-shaped fortress, Fort Snelling, on the former Dakota land on the bluffs above the junction of the Mississippi and Minnesota Rivers.

Like the British before them, the U.S. government wanted to control the fur trade and other river traffic. They also hoped to halt warfare between the Dakota and Ojibwa tribes, so settlers could safely move into the territory. Explorers, mapmakers, and census takers soon began to use Fort Snelling as a base of operations in the area.

In 1823, the U.S. government sent Major Stephen H. Long and a large group of military men through the valleys of the Mississippi, Minnesota, and Red Rivers. Long and his men visited Dakota villages and counted the population. They estimated that the total number of Dakota in the area had dwindled from nearly fifty thousand in the 1600s to about fifty-seven hundred people.

In 1825, the U.S. government convinced the Dakota and Ojibwa to sign a treaty creating a boundary between their lands. By assigning land to each tribe, they cleared the way for each tribe to give up rights to the land in the future. Fort Snelling was completed the same year this treaty was signed and became the first permanent U.S. settlement in the area.

John Jacob Astor and his American Fur Company led the American advance into Minnesota.

Life at Fort Snelling

Fort Snelling was the most important military post on the upper Mississippi. A group of settlers known as the Selkirkers lived safely within the walls of the fortress. The Dakota and Ojibwa came to the fort to trade. Soldiers at the fort enforced U.S. laws, inspecting the goods of all traders on the rivers.

By this time steamboats were carrying settlers and supplies up the river to the fort. During the long Minnesota winters, however, the rivers froze and boats could not reach the fort. The nearest town was three hundred

Fort Snelling was the most important military and trading post on the upper Mississippi.

miles away, so mail and supplies were delivered to the fort by dogsled. In the winter of 1826, however, the weather was so bad that no mail reached the fort for five months.

In the summer, the soldiers changed the landscape around the fort completely. They built roads throughout the area along with a sawmill, a flour mill, and a gristmill at nearby Saint Anthony Falls. They planted hundreds of acres of crops, brought in farm animals, and cut down trees for firewood.

Agents of the American Fur Company built more trading posts and military posts near Dakota villages in the area, and everybody gathered at Fort Snelling to trade. U.S. soldiers, fur traders, missionaries, and government officials set up homes near the posts.

American settlers soon began moving to the area looking for land to farm. When the settlers cut down the forests, game animals became scarce and the fur trade was affected. In the west, when ancient hunting

Some Dakota gave up their vast homelands and settled on small American-style farms.

grounds were turned into small farms, the buffalo began to disappear.

The Dakota depended on these animals, as well as the native plants and herbs, to live. They asked the traders, missionaries, and government officials to protect their rights to the land. Instead, government officials tried to persuade the Dakota to give up their vast homelands and settle on small American-style farms.

The Dakota and Ojibwa Treaties

In 1837, the U.S. Army threatened to destroy the Dakota people unless they signed a treaty giving up rights to about five thousand square miles of land east of the Mississippi. The same year, the Ojibwa were forced to sign a treaty surrendering the ancient pine forests in east-central Minnesota to loggers. In exchange the tribes were promised **trust funds**, medical aid, livestock, farm equipment, and teachers for farming to be sent from Washington, D.C.

Many of these goods never arrived, and those that did were often late and of poor quality. Products promised to the tribes were plundered by thieves on the long road between Washington and Minnesota.

The promised money was sent to local government agents in charge of Indian affairs. But many of the agents were dishonest, and most of the money was not used in ways described in the treaty. And when the funds did reach the tribes, local American traders raised their prices and drastically overcharged the Native Americans for goods.

After the treaty was signed, American missionary activity increased among the Dakota. But the Dakota did not wish to give up their religion or allow their children to be **segregated** from their families in religious boarding schools.

Meanwhile, the treaties allowed Saint Paul to become a steamboat port downstream from Saint Anthony Falls. The town of Stillwater on the Saint Croix River and the town of Saint Anthony (present-day Minneapolis) on the Mississippi River began to emerge as local centers for lumber operations.

Saint Paul became a steamboat port downstream from Saint Anthony Falls (pictured).

The Lumberjacks

Steamboats made it easy for the lumberjacks to travel to Minnesota on the waterways connected to the Mississippi River. The treaties of 1837 opened the region's lush pine forests to a flood of loggers who had previously been chopping down trees along the riverbanks in Maine. When the lumberjacks arrived, they found two-thirds of the region covered with virgin white pine trees more than one hundred feet high. Never before had these forests heard the ringing of steel axes and saws.

When the spring came, streams swelled, carrying pine logs to sawmill towns.

An early painting of Pig's Eye, which would grow to become Saint Paul, Minnesota's capital.

All through the long Minnesota winters, lumber-jacks cut down trees in the vast forests. The trees were cut into sections, dragged by horses to nearby streams, and stamped with a company mark. When the snow melted and the spring rains came, the streams swelled and carried the pine logs down the river to sawmills in Stillwater, Winona, and Saint Anthony.

The logging companies took all the logs they could. The rivers were often jammed with thousands of logs on their way to the sawmills to be cut into boards. For a time, Minneapolis became the biggest sawmilling center in the world. From there, the Mississippi River carried the lumber to be sold in growing cities such as Saint Louis and New Orleans.

The Pioneers

According to a well-known saying of the time, the plow follows the ax. Where the towering pines once stood, farmers were now able to plow up the land to plant crops. By the 1830s, a rush of pioneers were flooding into the logged areas to build farms.

In 1839, Swiss, Scotch, and French immigrants from Canada camped near where the Mississippi and Minnesota Rivers meet at Fort Snelling. One of the **squatters**, a retired fur trader named Pierre "Pig's Eye" Parrant, began to sell moonshine whiskey. Military officers at the fort were disturbed by the drunken rowdy behavior of the squatters, and banished them to an area that is now downtown Saint Paul.

In his new location, Pig's Eye Parrant's tavern served liquor to Native Americans as well as fur trappers, soldiers, and other pioneers. The area became known as Pig's Eye Landing, as it was the last place a steamboat could stop before the water became too shallow for navigation. Crowds poured into Pig's Eye saloon whenever a steamboat docked, greeting the newcomers and listening to the latest news from the rest of the world.

Eventually, the town called Pig's Eye would grow and become the city of Saint Paul, the capital of Minnesota.

Chapter Four

From Territory to State

T he activities of traders, loggers, and farmers increased in 1848, when neighboring Wisconsin became the thirtieth state admitted to the United States of America.

To respond to the needs of the settlers in Minnesota, fur traders, lumbermen, and merchants met at the Stillwater Convention in August 1848. In their one-day meeting, the self-appointed **delegates** named Henry H. Sibley, the regional director of the American Fur Company, to represent the Minnesota area in Congress. Since Sibley was not democratically elected, Congress had some doubts about the legality of his status. Nonetheless it allowed him to introduce new laws calling for the creation of Minnesota Territory.

The Minnesota Territorial Act became law on March 3, 1849. The territory, which extended west into present-day North and South Dakota, was nearly twice as large as the present state of Minnesota. Saint Paul became the capital of the territory. Alexander Ramsey, a Pennsylvania lawyer, became the first territorial governor.

Many names were suggested for the new territory, including Chippewa, Itasca, Jackson, and Washington. Finally it was agreed that the name of the new territory would be Minnesota, the Dakota word for "sky-tinted water."

The first territorial census, taken in the summer of 1849, reported only 4,535 white Americans living in the territory. The total Native American population was estimated at twenty-five thousand. Ramsey and Sibley wanted more land for European American farmers and began to negotiate treaties with the Dakota.

Henry H. Sibley called for the creation of the Minnesota Territory.

Alexander Ramsey became the first territorial governor of Minnesota.

The Dakota Treaties

In 1851 under the Treaty of Traverse des Sioux and the Treaty of Mendota, the Dakota sold their lands in Minnesota to the United States. In exchange for 28 million acres of some of the best farmland in the world, the Dakota were supposed to be given small reservation lands, a trust fund, cash payments, and other gifts. The Dakota leaders did not want to sign the treaty, because promises had been broken in the last treaty they signed. But when they were threatened with war they signed because they knew they could not win a war against the U.S. Army.

As before, promises of payments were not kept. The treaty had also tricked the Dakota into signing

The Dakota were tricked into selling their land under the Treaty of Traverse des Sioux.

"traders' papers" that said the tribe would pay traders for the debts of Dakota individuals. Many of the traders' claims against the Dakota were untrue. And many Dakota believed that the government had cooperated with the traders to cheat them.

Worst of all, the U.S. Senate eliminated the words in the treaty which promised to give small areas of land to the Dakota. President Franklin Pierce finally allowed the Dakota to live on small reservations until the American pioneers wanted the land. That did not take long—American pioneers had begun to set up farms on Dakota land before the treaty was even signed into law.

Prairie Farms

During the 1850s, thousands of pioneer farmers built small farms on the prairies of southwestern Minnesota. The land had already been cleared by the Dakota hunters who had set wildfires in earlier centuries to renew the grazing lands of the buffalo. As such, trees for building houses were scarce on the prairie. The pioneer farmers built their homes out of sod, the top layer of hardened dirt held together by prairie grass. Tree branches were used to strengthen the sod walls and roofs, which the farmers covered with mud and hay. Farmers worked together to build larger buildings such as barns.

Farmers harvested their crops by hand with a long blade called a scythe. Using this tool, however, a farmer

Thousands of pioneer farmers built small farms on the prairies of southwestern Minnesota.

could only harvest about two acres of crops in one day. Because of this pioneer farms were very small.

Men, women, and children all worked in the fields to plant and harvest the crops. As the years passed, farmers perfected their planting methods and small farms were able to grow a surplus of food. This extra grain was milled into flour and sold. In 1854, the first commercial flour mill opened at Saint Anthony Falls.

Meanwhile, East Coast newspapers wrote stories about Minnesota, the good prairie farmland, plentiful timber, and fresh water. Settlers began to flock to the area to set up their own farms. Dozens of flour mills were built to utilize the power of Minnesota's rivers. Minneapolis soon grew into the largest flour-milling city in the world.

Statehood

By 1856, the government had sold more than a million acres of Minnesota land, mostly to immigrants from Germany, Ireland, and Scandinavia. The population of Minnesota expanded from about forty thousand in 1853 to one hundred fifty thousand in 1857. The population increase led to numerous wishes to become a state. Henry M. Rice, who had succeeded Sibley as the territorial delegate to congress, led the effort.

In 1856, Rice introduced laws in congress that would help Minnesota become a state. In 1857 he won large federal land grants to encourage the construction of a railroad network in Minnesota. One-fifth of all the land in Minnesota was given to railroad companies. Saint

Paul, the capital city, and nearby Minneapolis were to be the important centers of the new railroads, which would help the farmers bring their goods to market.

In 1857, one hundred fifty thousand American settlers lived in the Territory of Minnesota. That year, a **convention** was held to write a state **constitution**. At that time, heated arguments took place over whether each new state should allow slavery, which was still legal in the United States. Differences over the slavery issue so divided the Minnesota convention that they drafted two different constitutions. After five weeks of arguments in the summer of 1857, a committee agreed upon a compromise constitution.

In 1857, one-fifth of Minnesota was given to railroad companies to build a railroad network.

After a long debate in Congress, Minnesota entered the Union on May 11, 1858.

Although some of the first European settlers in Minnesota owned slaves, many freed their slaves when they arrived in the territory and slavery was very rare by the time Minnesota was ready to become a state. When it seemed that Kansas Territory would enter the Union as a slave state, pro-slavery Southern congressmen allowed Minnesota to enter as a free state, where slavery would be against the law.

Voters overwhelmingly approved the constitution in the general election of October 13, 1857, in which the first state officials were also chosen. After a long debate in the U.S. Congress and active opposition from slave-state congressmen, Minnesota entered the Union on May 11, 1858, as the thirty-second state.

Facts About Minnesota

State motto: "Star of the North" or "L'Étoile du Norde" in French

State nicknames: "North Star State," "Land of 10,000 Lakes," "Gopher State"

State song: "Hail, Minnesota"

State capital: Saint Paul

State flower: a rare wildflower, the pink and white lady's slipper, which can live as long as one hundred years

State bird: the common loon

State tree: the Norway pine, also known as the red pine, which can grow up to one hundred feet tall

State gem: Lake Superior agate

State fish: walleye

State grain: wild rice

Wild plants: aster, bird's-foot violet, blazing star, bulrush, goldenrod, honeysuckle, Indian ricegrass, lady's slipper, prairie phlox, sweet fern, thimbleberry, trailing arbutus, water lily, wintergreen

Trees: ash, aspen, balsam, beech, birch, black walnut, elm, fir, maple, oak, pine, poplar, spruce

Birds: bald eagle, blackbird, duck, falcon, loon, meadowlark, owl, pheasant, sparrow, woodpecker, wren

Animals: badger, beaver, black bear, bobcat, fox, frog, gopher, gray wolf, moose, opossum, otter, porcupine, raccoon, skunk, squirrel, turtle, white-tailed deer

Stars of the North: Eugenie M. Anderson, Charles Bender, Patty Berg, Robert Bly, Warren E. Burger, Chief Little Crow, William O. Douglas, Bob Dylan, F. Scott Fitzgerald, Wanda Gág, Judy Garland, J. Paul Getty, Jessica Lange, Sinclair Lewis, William W. Mayo, Eugene McCarthy, Walter Mondale, Alan C. Page, Prince, Winona Ryder, Charles M. Schulz, Elaine Stately

Agriculture and livestock: apples, beef, corn, dairy, hogs, soybeans, sugar beets, turkey, vegetables, wheat

Fishing: carp, catfish, lake trout, pike

Manufacturing: chemicals, computers, food products, machinery, metal products, paper products, printed materials, scientific instruments, wood products

Mining: clay, granite, gravel, iron ore, limestone, peat, sand

Glossary

constitution: laws that guide governments

convention: a formal meeting of delegates of a political party

delegate: a person who represents a U.S. territory in the House of Representatives

detachment: military troops with a special mission or duty

fortress: a large, strong, permanent military shelter that often includes a town

monopoly: control of products or sales by one group

negotiate: to meet with others in order to reach an agreement

segregate: to separate from others in a group

squatter: one who settles on land without having a legal claim

trust fund: money held by one person or group to be paid to another.

For Further Exploration

Raymond Bial, *The Sioux*. New York: Benchmark Books, 1999. Examines the origins, beliefs, language, and culture of the Sioux, also known as the Dakota Indians.

Jeffrey D. Carlson, *A Historical Album of Minnesota*. Brookfield, CT: The Millbrook Press, 1993. A history of Minnesota from before the Europeans arrived to the present, highlighting the influence of farming, industry, railroads, wars, and the depression on the state.

Megan O'Hara, *Frontier Fort: Fort Life on the Upper Mississippi, 1826*. Mankato, MN: Blue Earth Books, 1998. Provides a look at the history and importance of Fort Snelling and describes what life was like for its inhabitants.

Gordon Regguinti, *The Sacred Harvest: Ojibway Wild Rice Gathering*. Minneapolis, MN: Lerner Publications, 1992. Glen Jackson Jr., an eleven-year-old Ojibway Indian in northern Minnesota, goes with his father to harvest wild rice, the sacred food of his people.

Index